I0836056

Pneuma

Pneuma

poems by

Jennifer Lothrigel

Liquid Light Press

Premium Chapbook First Edition

ISBN-10: 0-9985487-2-3

ISBN-13: 978-0-9985487-2-2

Liquid Light Press

poetry for the heart

www.liquidlightpress.com

Book Design: M. D. Friedman
Cover Photos: Jennifer Lothrigel

Contents

To Lift Darkness

Rise.
Rise gently.
Rise like buoyant limbs in a celestial ocean,
like there is no other destination.

Be a body of dreams
and wild bushes.
Be dreams that snuck out your bedroom window last night
and ran naked through the damp woods.
Be the shiver and the air breathing together at your skin's surface.

Be the wild bush with glowing edges
and abundant plump berry offerings.
Be living kindness.

Be mindful of the way infinity rests her mind
on your shoulder.
Rise up with a cloak of invisible plush blankets
softening your arrival.

Rest into the humble imperfect moment
and let it devour you.

Wholly fearless of your ego death,
become something other than what you were yesterday.

Become the fragrance of the white sage leaf lifting itself into morning light.
Become the impossible, unknown, incapable, insignificant thing
that shakes free one more bit of transcendence from the dreaming
Spirit of the Universe.

Pneuma

Escape temporal mind,
breath defies gravity.
That which thinks inside of me—
is poetic empty space
migrating with the morning wind.

Inspirited belly
dreams of surrendering battles,
of giving up her ghosts.

Dissolve limitations,
grow lotus flowers
on their bones.

Flow at the edge of
losing myself.

Stillness,
light,
the Universe,
we're sung of kaleidoscopic notes,
breath-written,
unopinionated.

Exhale,
a lineage of listening trees
already forgave your woes.

Body \\ Temple

A prismatic temple
where indigo fountains
proudly display their
wished upon pennies.

Here, the ground re-members a new past
and the unknown journey ahead
is a weightless language gliding on the wind.

Here you will accept your loneliness,
while the sound of light fills the room of your body.

You are holy water,
pressed to the third eye,
knowing of no other possible moment.

Here you will redefine lost
as the place
where you tether your incandescent skin to stillness.

Questions for an Ascended Light Being

How do I find the courage for reincarnation
when my free spirit is banished from her home?

How do I stay calm
when I'm in the belly of the underworld?

I'm just wondering about salvation,
during the dark season of the soul.
How might I seek illumination again,
when the hardened thorns of deceased roses
have possessed my womanhood?

Last night I wanted to harvest my longing for three dimensional life
as I floated against the backdrop of billions of galaxies,
but I just couldn't.

All I know is that the stars
were full of yearning,
and I lost myself to the mystery of being weightless.

Prayer Like a River

I went to the creek
to hold my hidden sorrows

cupped in my hands
beneath the clear water
near the mossy edge

until my body
felt free of obligation
to anyone,
except the smooth blue rocks
beneath my feet.

The stream wrinkled up
the time-written messages
across my skin.

Weightlessly danced by rushing currents,
I lifted my hands to my heart center,
matched up the life line of each palm,
and pressed them together,

then fell my forehead to the tips of my fingers
and wrote a new destiny.

In the Absence of My Infinity

Call me speckled pebble
in the moonlight,
the moisture slick on my smooth body.
Call me incense smoke
dancing across a red stained glass window.
Call me unafraid of losing myself.

Call to the mediator of impermanence,
digging her long fingernails into resistance.
I want to hold on
like strangling vines,
like the haunting ghost
flickering bedroom lights.

Who am I in the absence of infinity?
The overstayed lover
reliving her abandonment issues,
the foggy morning
rolling itself into nothingness,
the blue tide reaching towards the shore
crashing
over and over again?

Call me void of belonging
to one thing,
call me the dripping nectar
of a swollen blood orange
drying sticky to goose-bumped skin
in the thick of winter's reign.

I am the moon howling back,
inaudible to human ears,
yet deeply fulfilled.

Unruined Heartbeat

I ask my body to soften,
meet ground to bone,
unfurl.

Pardon loneliness from spinal fluid,
from childhood years of rounding inward
like leaves
on an unwatered houseplant.

Unravel muscles
from untouchable memories.
Knead stiff sorrow
with hands of light.

I listen again
to my lucent,
unruined
heartbeat,
longing to be born again
of primordial seas.

Tall Grass Mysteries

I want to
become lost in a nurtured forest,
bent by northern winds,
while morning dew lures me closer to the ground,
glowing and all wet.

I want to understand the meaning of
becoming wider with each year,
of digging my roots into a million years of stories.

I want to know how Silence offers her patience to
the grasshopper who pleads for his lover,
as she divinely carves out the pause between sounds,
perfectly timed
to the infinite cosmic arrangement.

I want to know the moist blades of grass
intimately,
the way it feels to be the light in their limbs,
at the very moment they release their breath.

Psyche Is a Monarch Butterfly

Half mythological creature,
half vulnerable body and wings.

Do you want to find your place in the world?
Does the impermanence of third dimension reality
lure you towards some charted destiny?

Or do you want to flutter your marvelous wings,
silently pulsing your body
up and down
against the sunlight splattered air?

Forget about migration.
Revel in beautiful orange and black painted bodies
keeping each other warm,
stacked upon one another
high up in the eucalyptus tree,
resting before the long flight.

The Moon

Who was holding who?
The moon rested her curved backside
atop my crown.
I became a vortex of visions,
and fertile femininity.

The night was dark and
the wind howled around me,
sonically inviting my
body to awaken.

I felt the tug of sea creatures
with their claws
pinching my legs,
my sheer green nightgown
glowing as it blew
behind me,
reaching toward the deep black sky.

I was torn between
two strange invitations.
One, to wash away my sins,
and one to dive into them
and free their pearls.

Kali, Save Me

I am sitting here holding all of Kali's hands,
skulls of men she has eaten clank around her neck.

Om krim kalikayai namah

Destroy my loveless demons.

Make moksha for repeating patterns.

I will not be abandoned again.
Eat the head off the woman who seeks home
within distant lovers.

Circle back to my first breath.
Arrive out of the womb,
into a room where everyone
knows how to love me.

Hold Kali's hands.
Destroy the aftermath of unwanted.
You did not come scrounging for leftovers.
You came to flesh out the untethered exquisite
soul inside of you.

Arriving into the World of My Body

I arrived like a river
brushing up against muddy edges,
softening edgy stones along my way.

I arrived within a body and I became
my own body,
and I became the bodiless essence of
night-light glowing on my skin.

I became the dense meaning behind
letting go and
the mountain's version of atonement,
the still existence of standing in the bright of high noon
with my shadow harsh
for all to see.

I entered unsuppressed,
and like the silent woods receiving an unexpected guest,
quickly hid away my secret creatures.

I greeted the atmosphere's breath with reverie
and bowed my spine
to an inescapable longing for balance.

Somehow, I allowed my sorrow to be weightless
and drift through multiple realities,
remembered how to arrive like a feather.

Remembered there were constellations in my bones
weaving ancient stories
with a newly formed
stable cosmos.

The Lessened Hard

(A sermon on perfectionism in the case of women's bodies)

Who wished you might be
the lady cobra
slithering through their thighs
while starving for a meal?

Rather,
be undulating woman
with her venom flowing thick,
the well-fed conquering She.

Whoever asked your stomach be flat
has never tasted ecstasy
in the ladle of their tongue,
has never held a woman's edges
in their palms
and felt an eternal mystery
newly arriving.

Whoever unloved the plummeting- meteor- carved scars
that marked your surface;
curse their misunderstanding of otherworldly.

So you were reshaped by inescapable sorrow,
so you were bent and burnt and marked with red Xs.
Tell them how you slip
your heart into nothingness
and return
dancing to the sound of
wild mustangs
stampeding across a great valley floor.

Buddha in the Rubble

If I fall apart,
I'll dig through the bones of the wreckage,
find my wish granting remains,
try hard to break off the larger half.

I'll find Buddha laughing in the rubble,
feel his belly quake
with enlightened reverie
for fate's dark side.

I'll be the catastrophic dust,
rising up
silver-lined,
as it refracts shards of failure
and drifts its way into a oneness with the pink horizon.

Out of the Labyrinth

The night before I was born
Ariadne gave me a red ball of yarn
that slowly unraveled for 99 years.
On the day it revealed its starting point,
I held tightly the tip of braided threads
to my belly and
traveled through time,
my body, feather drifting
in a giant, cosmic womb.
Stars were weaving through my auric field and
I listened to the hum of divine madness
with no loneliness in my heart.
I became stillness and
each essential thing my heart had clung too.

Body, Breath, Longing

I breathe like
soft white linen curtains
undulating in the afternoon breeze,
sunlit and content.

My body is a receptacle
for chosen reality,
pores sung to
by a whispering breeze,

sometimes an intrusive
soul scattering gust.

I'm learning how to yearn wide open
like windows do,
aroused by the light.

I am a primitive mystery
entranced with the continuum
of human skin,

the conflux of delicate sensation
in a harsh world.

Ancestor Hips

These hips
hold ancestral emotions—
deep tissue release.

There's a poet in here,
great-grandmother's love letters
worn and tattered
never sent,

hidden unfolded words
still crying when I open my legs.

Caress with lavender.
Shout from the pelvic floor,
rumbled pain bellowing
into celestial sky.

I came to flesh them out.
Spin a new range of motion
from grandmother's iridescent tears.

The unresolved
teetering at the edge of a shared humble vision,
longing like a quantum river
pushing wider open
to be received by the infinite dark sea.

Note from Higher Self

Dear Dreaming Spirit,

When did you become afraid of letting go?

Your pain body is a mythological
bird flying you back home.
Hold reins loosely,
root down your backbone,
slip into the mystery of flight.

There is medicine in visible breath
hot on the Soul's mirror.
Exhale
and claim
your divine muscle memory.

Your living flesh is a ritual
induced enactment of peaceful bones
floating through ether,
timeless,
still human,
with indefinite destiny.

The unnamable center
of your being is bonded to
the wild ever after.

Tread your luminosity
carefully, ever
in pursuit of the wild,
untangled path.

Surrender

The leaves will all fall off
sometime around December
despite their feelings of intimacy
with branches that held them so perfectly through the cold nights
and wild winds.

They will fall,
appearing to float gracefully
as if guided to a purposeful landing.

They will sacrifice their bodies,
fall apart,
become building materials for worker ants,
become the rich soil womb
for soft roots,
become has-been autumn leaves,
lose all claims to identifiable forms,
rest selflessly
amongst stardust and other fallen beauties
in a brown indistinguishable pile of dirt.

Web of Light

We are each
one point of connection
illusioned by separateness
in the glistening web of light.
Collective chariot,
high vibrational vessel
of infinite being
pulled by a silvery
umbilical cord reaching us
towards the divine center
of the Great Mother's heart.

Dreaming Goddess of Malta

As you are ever connected to the deep night,
sacred and holy,
dream peace for us.

Ask the Dark Mother
shown of stars,
faceless in her beauty,
to open the portal
of self-compassion
to those whose scars
keep them hidden.

Dream fierce courage for us,
that our individuality
be met with embrace
and empowering acceptance.

Dream us awakened wisdom,
visible kindness
standing at the entrance
to a great sacred world.

The Keeper of the Web

One drop of water
or rustle of wind
makes the whole web listen.

And there she is in her
long white gown
refastening its corners
to the edges of the world.

Every memory and dream
ever ignited or lost
is alive in the intricate grid
of her finely woven Universe.

Pieces always come undone,
broken
with someone or
something left feeling
disconnected from their lineage.

So she mends,
eternally,
one sticky strand at a time.

About the Author

Jennifer Lothrigel is a poet, artist and healer residing in the San Francisco Bay area. Her work has been published in *Trivia - Voices of Feminism, Narrative Northeast, Poetry Quarterly, The Bitter Oleander Press, The Tishman Review, Corvus Review* and elsewhere.

Visit her online at *www.JenniferLothrigel.com.*

Acknowledgments

"Prayer Like A River," published in *Aji Magazine*

"Unruined Heartbeat," published in *Heartbeat Lit Journal*

"Tall Grass Mysteries," published in *The Bitter Oleander Press*

"Psyche Is a Monarch Butterfly," published in *Five Poetry Magazine*

"The Moon," published in *Slink Chunk Press*

"Arriving into the World of My Body," published in *Five Poetry Magazine*

"Buddha in the Rubble," published in *Five Poetry Magazine*

"Out of the Labyrinth," published in *Poetry Quarterly*

"Body, Breath, Longing," published in *The Haight Ashbury Journal*

"The Keeper of the Web," published in *Fickle Muses*

Other Books from Liquid Light Press

All books are available directly from *liquidlightpress.com* or from any of the current major global distribution channels including Amazon, Barnes and Noble, the iBookstore and the Ingram Catalog.

- ♥ *Leaning Toward Whole* **by M. D. Friedman (2011)** – Explores the poignant and personal. Also available as a groundbreaking multimedia enhanced e-book.
- ♥ *The Miracle Already Happening – Everyday Life with Rumi* **by Rosemerry Wahtola Trommer (2011)** – A special collection of poems full of heart, humor, peace and wisdom.
- ♥ *Spiral* **by Lynda La Rocca (2012)** – A compelling poetic and melodic discourse of the persistent cravings and fears inside of each of us.
- ♥ *From the Ashes* **by Wayne A. Gilbert (2012)** – A true masterpiece that gnaws at the heart with universal appeal.
- ♥ *ah* **by Rachel Kellum (2012)** – This poetry has a simplicity and clarity that cuts to the core of being human.
- ♥ *Catalyst* **by Jeremy Martin (2012)** – *Catalyst* may just launch you on a fiery ride into yourself.
- ♥ *Of Eyes and Iris* **by Erika Moss Gordon (2013)** – Beautiful yet poignant in its simplicity.
- ♥ *Your House Is Floating* **by Susan Whitmore (2013)** – As smooth, crisp and satisfying as olive oil on fresh garden greens.
- ♥ *Nowhere Near Morning* **by Jeffrey M. Bernstein (2013)** – An intimate embrace of what it means to be alive.
- ♥ *Harmonica* **by Cecele Allen Kraus (2014)** – *Harmonica* bristles with a shimmering music that heals the heart.
- ♥ *Surf Sounds* **by Roger Higgins (2014)** – Expertly crafted and superbly written, pulsing with the tides of the soul.
- ♥ *Black-Footed Country* **by Lindsay Wilson (2015)** – Like eating an artichoke, there are layers within thorny layers, each one more tender and subtle until you feast on the heart inside.
- ♥ *The Dice Throwers* **by Douglas Cole (2015)** – *The Dice Throwers* shines like a flashlight across the gritty dark alleys of the American soul, turning shattered glass into diamonds.
- ♥ *Lessons on Sleeping Alone* **by Megan E. Freeman (2015)** – While easily accessible, Megan's elegant writing is complexly layered with hard-won common sense and clarity.
- ♥ *The Offering* **by Eleanor Kedney (2016)** – A masterful, poetic tapestry woven from what makes us human.
- ♥ *This Town, Poems of Correspondence* **by Kyle Laws & Jared Smith (2017)** – This gritty collaboration on small town America between two of Colorado's finest poets will hit you where you live.

www.ingramcontent.com/pod-product-compliance
Lightning Source LLC
La Vergne TN
LVHW050947080826
845145LV00004B/1441

* 9 7 8 0 9 9 8 5 4 8 7 2 2 *